THE
CONSCIENCE
OF
TREES

THE
CONSCIENCE
OF
TREES

SELECTED POEMS

Zoltán Böszörményi

TRANSLATED FROM THE HUNGARIAN
BY PAUL SOHAR

RAGGED SKY PRESS
PRINCETON, NEW JERSEY

Published by Ragged Sky Press
270 Griggs Drive
Princeton, NJ 08540
www.raggedsky.com

Paintings on cover and section start pages © Botond Részegh, 2017, acrylic on paper, 35 x 25 cm.

ISBN (pbk.): 978-1-933974-29-3

Library of Congress Control Number: 2018943160

This book has been composed in Neu Haas Unica Pro and Cambria

Printed on acid-free paper. ∞

Printed in the United States of America

ZOLTÁN BÖSZÖRMÉNYI

"Zoltán Böszörményi's voice rises pure and truth-filled to join the poets not alone of middle-Europe, but of the world. This is a poetry whose DNA is sourced in the struggles and rebellions of a Hungarian past, but which carries forward to join in a philosophical chorale enriched by place, ideas and love itself. The tone is uncompromising, sometimes ironic, and never overstated. The poet writes, 'My poem is a passing footprint/in the soft sands of your soul'; then invites the reader to make space for his words. An inheritor of the message of the great Attila József, he presents the struggle between self and society, between class and soul, with an almost conversational energy. And yet, he is conscious of the necessary inventions: of the fairytale of childhood with all its complexities and difficulties, and of the huge, symbolic 'toddler' capable of whacking someone's soul 'into docile domestic stock.' These are visionary poems written by a pilgrim soul whose poetic is enriched by the voices of the classical past. We are honored to witness this gifted sensibility."

—*Mary O'Donnell, January 10th, 2018*

CONTENTS

The Dust of My Existence

The Mirage of Our Fate

ABOUT THE AUTHOR

Zoltán Böszörményi (1951–), Romanian-Hungarian poet and novelist, was born and educated in the Transylvanian-Hungarian area of Romania. He had literary ambitions, but as a young poet he was harassed by the communist authorities of that time. He had no choice but to escape, eventually finding a new home in Canada, where he graduated from York University in philosophy and got a job with an advertising agency. After the fall of communism, he went back to Romania to start a publishing firm, Irodalmi Jelen Könyvek (Literature Today) and to resume his literary career. In addition to several volumes of poetry, he published three novels in Hungary, two of which also found print in Sohar's English translation: *Far from Nothing* (Exile Editions, Canada, 2006) and *The Club at Eddie's Bar* (Phaeton Press, Ireland, 2013). His third novel, *The Refugee* (2018), came out in Berlin in German translation. Presently he divides his time between Transylvania and Barbados, between the business of running the publishing house (which includes the influential Hungarian literary magazine *Irodalmi Jelen*, online and in print) and work on his own novels and poetry.

This poetry is quite current in approach and content but also reflects that special Eastern European angst that has accumulated in the collective consciousness of the region over its turbulent history. However, the alternation between free verse and formal style is entirely due to the fact that Hungarian language allows for an infinite variety of rhyme pairs and any form of meter, and much of contemporary Hungarian poetry is still produced in conventional form. For this book, the selected poems were grouped not by style but by theme; the first part containing meditative poems, the second part devoted to personal/lyrical poems, and the third to poems inspired by or dedicated to other poets and writers. Various styles and forms are represented in each cycle; only outstanding quality and significant content were considered for inclusion.

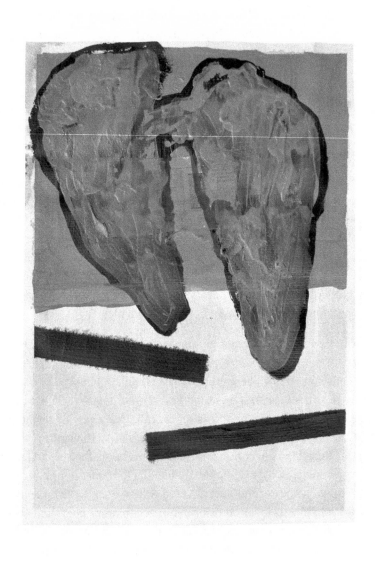

THE ELLIPSE
OF
MERCY

LEGLESS TIME

(A lábatlan idő)

A thing, that's what man is.
He gets rounded up, trained, put to toil.
The laws of the material world rule over him.
After all, he's the universe,
mushrooming matter
intent on maintaining balance.

Matter is forgetful,
unlike a mattress.
The bed where once a man slept
preserves his spatial body print,
a heavenly hand glazes it with light
to make it more visible, that place of rest,
in case our gaze should land on it,
to the amazement of the stars.

In blind space
legless time does a handstand and walks off.

THE POEM DIDN'T JOIN THE CLASS STRUGGLE*
(A vers nem lett osztályharcos)

(the poem dropped out didn't join the class struggle
toured Paris saw Endre Ady** and went to track
down Pushkin in Moscow driven by an urge to juggle
the view of his untamed face
in search of liberty and love
until daylight turned black above
an obsession with groins, desires and loud memories
carried the city on shoulders and hips
rattling steel chains perhaps mine
and stopped on the corner with bloodless lips)

you cried out: "go join the class struggle!
together with the masses you'll rise!"
only in the meantime classes got fuzzy
and I'm nowhere in the era I wore off
I was stumbling in thickening fog
all my efforts were for nothing
believe me the word did not make an iron fist

all the loaves of bread have been eaten
the kasha cooked
the milk is gone
even though stores are stacked with merchandise
replete with all kinds of goods
just like before one half the world
doesn't get enough to eat

no one is hungry for words
but wants novelty undefined

the taste of erupting joy
the scent of coriander
the fire of rebellion
the moment when they don't have to
compromise with anyone or anything
and there's no need for lies

is the face in the mirror the same
as the one looking in it?

all mirrors lie
the moment gives birth to a crippled era
sandbagging words
saving them for tomorrow
and a safe place
for the nonexistent soul
to survive the winter

better speak of the nothing

the world of time has frayed into fog
the dancer on tightrope
looks with awe at thick reality
keeps dancing
dance-stepping
the deep chasm is gaping at his steps
with a big open mouth
and the stones catch on fire
if his step should stray

nothing but good intentions are left of the creek
the grass
the succulent skin of afternoons

the palpable dreams
the scattered wonders
the ratcheted joy of expectations

today the public morals of trees are impeccable
today there's no protest for or against the government
today the vultures of war are screeching over us
the ghosts of fear mount a rally in densely packed waves
a white flag is fluttering on top of the Acropolis
China has bought up our desires at a low price
now they're sold for pennies on the global stock exchange

poem
do you see the future?

why should you have joined the class struggle
when words planted in our soil produce only chaff
your cheeks sting from the slaps delivered by liars
the smiles of hypocrites burnish the sunshine
while bitter clouds sail the sky of your awareness
you have a feeling all's about to fall
common sense would not bump into a solid wall
haystacks of light would not gather in the sky
oh what a precious ashtray the soul can make

(and you're accused of not fighting hard enough
you dropped your tools your faith your inspiration
even the flame and only heaped imprecation
till you fell as if hit by meteors from above)

poem
do you see the future?

the creator is laid back in the bed of space the dream is nil
the shallow night has bled into mist it's flying in your face

with algae rocking in it as it wiggles to you on the smile of veins
stitch yourself with that to ancient skies and cast your eyes at me
although it lets all accessories of desire go to waste your muscles bind
I ask the fear that listens to its strings to come stand with me on a cliff
and make believe that you're again living off the power of today

poem
do you see your future?

*Attila József (1905–1937) the modern Hungarian poet of the highest renown in world
literature. The title refers to a line "poem, go, join the class struggle ..." from his poem
"The Socialists."
**Endre Ady (1877–1919), seminal Hungarian poet of the 20th century and farsighted
journalist. His articles on culture and literature urged progress in his backward country;
he often visited Paris and wrote several iconic poems on these occasions.

WELCOME VISITORS

(Kedves városnézők)

Welcome visitors to our town
this is Haydn Square
perhaps it's unnecessary to mention
it was named after Haydn even though
the composer never came near this place
but the town fathers had heard about him
and decided
to give this square Haydn's name
after all it sounds prestigious
the *ah* sound lends itself to lingering
with a soft aye to dissolve into need
I remind you in this fifty-thousand square meters
less sunshine is needed to be imported
from abroad (unfortunately the price of
oxygen doubled just last week) and fewer
glass bell jars are needed for the flowers
but as you can see we have a gorgeous view here
and with this the one minute scheduled for this stop
has expired we thank you for your patience and
wish you a good time for the rest of your stay with us

AND IT'S THE MONEY EVERYWHERE

(És mindenütt a pénz)

Shed your pilgrim robe, Virgil,

put on your Sunday best! You've put in your time serving Dante,

come now and sit with us! Let's survey the sky together!

It's getting late. The gates of hell are already closed.

Levites are guarding the walls of Florence,

keeping the night from entering.

Sit down beside me and let's daydream:

has the world progressed since Aristotle

or does history only go around in cycles,

repeating the same whirls everywhere?

Virtual windows open,

they wink at one another.

Dawn gives chase to the defeated army of dreams.

New plans preen themselves on the stone benches of light.

And it's the money everywhere.

A virtual world is sitting on the throne of filthy lucre,

with arms folded and a contemptuous smile on the lips.

(Virgil, let us recite a Sanskrit mantra.)

We're all dancing on a razor's edge and hardly

ever take notice if it's already too late for this or that,

the impermanent is permanently gone,

from time to time archives too are copied over

and over in line with the sponsor's taste. (I believe

even Aristotle was aware of that.)

Since nobody wanted it, and nobody had to die for it,

poetry has not become a major power

but the senseless suffering of those bent under their angst.

And it's the money everywhere.

We can't take a step without it.

(The mind piles moan on groan,

piles of nothingness whirl eddies in the stream of life.)

We're the prisoners of its gravitation.

The prognosis of our condition is hopeful; no one can hide

the secret of the universe, we bury it inside us.

Withered summers rest on our chests,

and we find sauna in social autocracy.

Thank Heaven, things are happening to us.

Happening, because we remain consistent:

stone, clay tablet, bone, silk, papyrus, paper, monitor,

stone, clay tablet, bone, silk . . .

suspicion the size of a white blood cell.

Sins can be forgiven. No need for the sinner to atone.

Hammurabi still says: *An eye for an eye.*

Pythagoras, Thales, Hippocrates, Archimedes.

A clear mind doesn't explain the world,

but the stars do.

Virgil, you do agree with me, don't you?

We're spying on the gods we've created.

On that one and only.

May that one never forsake us.

That's why we betray that one a thousand times and more.

(Okay, let's just say at least once a day.)

And it's the money everywhere.

Cannibals armed with capital.

Trees bearing noise and reed flowers deck the playing field of morals.

Let us protect the Boys of Pál Street!*

Even if in the West the situation of poetry has not improved.
(No better here.)
Track poetic feet with Argus eyes as long as they keep going
and don't gamble away the chance of survival,
like our forebears lost Hungary a hundred years ago.

*God save the Hungarians!***
... that government of the people, by the people, for the people ... ***

We warm up by summer's stove.
It doesn't matter how often, so long as
others too can get close to the fire.
And if they can't, congruencies bleed to death
on the battlefields of the everyday,
atavistic dreams adhere to the iron bars of obsessions,
and there's no solution for old solutions.
The tragic monomania of repetition,
and the forgettable unforgettable.

We'd gladly conquer other mountains even higher
than this just in order to behold this one's face,
because we've come here driven by the need to see
*what puts a smile on its cloud-covered gaze.****

And it's the money everywhere, isn't it?

---

*The title of a popular youth novel written by Ferenc Molnár (1878–1952), a Hungarian-
born dramatist and novelist who adopted American citizenship. He immigrated to
the United States to escape persecution of Hungarian Jews during World War II.
**From the Hungarian national anthem
***From Abraham Lincoln's Gettysburg Address
****From *Thus Spoke Zarathustra [Also sprach Zarathustra]* by Friedrich Nietzsche

FOREST AND FIELD
(Erdő, mező)

The social order of the forest is very distinct.
Full of piety and condescension.
Turns its head toward the sky in a showy way.
That's how it observes the surrounding world:
the field. Proud of its spectacular landscape.
From a bird's-eye view the forest readily lectures
on subjects the field should understand,
calls for freethinking and freedom,
protects the disadvantaged,
extends confidence and safety to the weak,
looks down upon the excitable and
always-complaining field that keeps
fomenting new and newer revolutions.
The forest doesn't want to struggle,
to falsify conscience and meaning,
to exchange ideas, but simply to go on living.
Its slogan: the diversity of the individual is
power, light and air.
Although it listens to new songs,
it enjoys the classics, the birthplace of music.
Plato, Shakespeare, Erasmus, Lao-Tse,
and the Orphic melodies. It keeps in touch
with Faulkner, Updike, Pynchon,
adores Nietzsche, Rilke
and all the Romantics.
The forest doesn't understand why the field seeks pity
just because it gets plowed, sprinkled with seeds,
the new vegetation peeled from its body every summer,
why? the field cries to bushes and bees, why

is it constantly robbed and kept enslaved?
(The philosophy of history tells us
the field is fine as it is, should be left in peace.)
The forest feels the same way, just as disadvantaged
as the field. Its word carries no more weight,
but is more disciplined, under better control,
more at peace,
its experiences more varied and vivid,
its leaves whisper humanist ideals,
its deeply planted roots deliver
the nectar of wisdom.
That's the source of its eudemonia.
New Order. New ambitions. New directions for imagination.
New way of seeing the world, the recognition
and evaluation of new possibilities.
The forest has no intention
of retouching the truth
but lets it stay where and the way it is,
in its natural order as determined by the laws of nature.
It shouldn't matter whether
we approach reality
from the forest or the field
so long as we follow nature's path to our given soul.

THE ELLIPSE OF MERCY

(Az irgalom ellipszise)

he made a will leaving wealth and fancy living
to someone else rather than family
lest they be tempted by social position
(haughty power)
later he expounded
to his wife and children
on the past (the wedding of time)
wheat spurting up fine blond sheaves
symbolizing the sublime

ellipse=$\{P|d(P,F_1)+d(P,F_2)=r_1+r_2=\text{constant}=2a>d(F_1;F_2)\}$*

    (Atheist ideology is called
    materialism. This religion is based on
    three dogmas: there's no such thing as soul,
    man is an animal, death is annihilation.)

he did not think what he was supposed to
(the stars split open the sky like a can of beans)
the injury of uncertainty in all things
(wind was whipping the silk of existence)

anxiety was of no help
in accepting the unacceptable
(the powerful coming from
the opposite direction on the road)
liberating mercy

---

* In mathematics, an *ellipse* is a curve in a plane surrounding two focal points such
that the sum of the distances to the two focal points is constant for every point on
the curve.

NIKOLA TESLA'S WHITE DOVE

(Nikola Tesla fehér galambja)

God's taken me into his confidence. In the form of a dove.
In the past few weeks he spent the mornings with me
in Central Park.
I fed bread crumbs to the bird
as if feeding delicious illusions to my soul.
He already knew that Doctor Wembly would visit me today
around ten this morning in the New Yorker Hotel,
in Room 3327.
He wears glasses, and before leaning over me,
he adjusts them on his nose
to better see death.
I'm just lying stretched out on the bed
covered with a sheet of dubious cleanliness
giving a green light for the death certificate to be written
by this unremarkable medico, but a rather jovial gentleman.
My desiccated body cannot be a pleasant sight,
but it doesn't take very long to determine the time of death.
He just hems and haws over me
as a member of the Supreme Court would do
finding fault with Marconi* in seventeen points.
In the adjacent room a radio can be heard ...
They still called it broadcasting, and it cost a fortune and no less
when the first announcer sat down with the microphone to address,
his clarion voice took to the sky and flew into its wilderness,
*to gain voice speaking to a listener—the test was a success!***

Curious indeed is the force that lets voice filter through walls!
My gaze is still fixed on the white dove, now gone several days.

The world is a noisy waiting room.
Everyone's in a hurry, in a tizzy and loud,
a curious manifestation of intelligence built of matter.
Under the clouds of Niagara
a rainbow swells its chest toward a placid sky.
Holly bush.

Doctor Wembly is still standing beside me.
I stare at him,
but not with the same disdainful look
with which I regarded Edison
when he was badmouthing alternating current,
yet *squealing transformers are*
suckling on the metallic nipples of generators.***

Time's white canvas is fluttering above me,
and in the neighboring room
the radio keeps blaring. . . .
Sometimes it disturbs us, sometimes machines can disturb it, too,
You can slip it into a pocket, but watch it, it can also pocket you.
In good weather the sound is loud and clear,
And sometimes even an old song may reappear . . . **
Without this fluttering sound
this universe around me could freeze up,
as it is I'm alone turning stiff like a cliff.

Doctor Wembly is ready to leave,
from the door, though, he glances back,
his lips crumbling words:
genius is one percent inspiration
and ninety-nine percent perspiration,****
and for farewell he shakes his head.

I watch him with disapproval,

wish he had quoted someone else,

but the door closes behind him,

and through the thin walls

a radio is blaring from the neighboring room.

My gaze is still fixed on the white dove,

now gone for several days.

*Guglielmo Marconi (1874–1937), Italian physicist, received the Nobel Prize for the discovery of the radio. The Supreme Court of the USA revoked the distinction from him in 1943, only a few months after the death of Nicola Tesla, who was posthumously awarded the patent.
**Dusán Sztevanovity (1945–), two quotes from his pop song "The Radio," LGT, 1977.
***Attila József (1905–1937), two lines quoted from the poem "Laborers."
****Thomas Alva Edison (1847–1931), proverbial quote.

OF THINGS

(Dolgokról)

Tie things to things, think that through!

Like it or not, things all tie themselves to you.

They're becoming a burden already.

You didn't ask for them? They cling to you

with some inexplicable mystical force

like a Schopenhauer thesis. (The premise.)

The spiral of the Milky Way (with a billion stars,

black holes, quasars and parallel galaxies in it)

takes two hundred and thirty thousand years

to spin around once,

and in the heart of one of its wings: our Solar System.

And on Planet Earth you are but a puny point.

Let this recognition raise your spirit,

if nothing else has.

ON WILLPOWER

(Az akaratról)

> The place where things came to exist is
> where they return on their extinction
> as a natural consequence of necessity.

You expect me to bow down before you
and celebrate you,
twisting the knife in the heart of thought
the way God used to twist mortality
in ours.
The raving joy of rebellion
smashes the fragile glass podium of the law
into a thousand shards!
This is what I celebrate,
the resistance.
The protest slogans fly from branch to branch,
they hide a bird among frigid-handed,
leaf-covered limbs.
Protest becomes the birdsong,
like life, more venturous,*
lives forever, like the flame that's
passed around from hand to hand.
True grit demands yet more;
like Love
that moves the sun and other stars.**
Under the weight of elemental forces
the branch of an oak may crack
but not the power of the will.

*Rainer Maria Rilke (1875–1926)
**Dante Alighieri (1265–1321), the last line of "The Divine Comedy"

THE FACE

(Az Arc)

Don't ask

what it was God used to create the world!

It'd be a waste of words.

According to the moral exegesis,

the study of creation makes those haughty

who ignore the examination of Midrash Aggadah

and the Midrash Halakha.

The gap between our finite knowledge

and the infinity of divine will is enormous.

The root cause of creation is love

that ended up enslaving us.

And yet, man's tree of life can bloom

if he's blessed with love.

The purpose of creation:

no such thing on the divine scale!

But think,

what is this unseemly eagerness,

this raw power

with which we want to expropriate God

who lives in us from the moment of conception?

What kind of a curse, what night is whirling

in our mind without letting us rest

until we see that face shine on us from the material fog?

We are this face.

HOW SMOOTHLY LIES CAN LIE
(Intimissimi)

How smoothly lies can lie to the world,
how convincingly to liars, too!
Reality catches up with us and arms us,
the mutating ones; the perceived injury
compresses a thousand volts in our veins.
They wave the lamps of Diogenes in front of us.
Let's see the dark, let the light wash our somber thoughts,
let it scrub them white!
Sanitation!

Some can see the trees in the wood.
Let the cunning soul fool himself as he will,
there's no way he can hurry up the future.
The future is us, we carry the future inside us,
and the constant want, the drudgery,
the jeers others heap upon us,
the pain of being dispossessed,
the glory and the tragedy of the fraud victim.
Fanaticism teaches a lesson.
(Winks at us if we arrive on time.)
The Facebook generation, they are activists,
they mobilize and elevate you:
If you come out at four this afternoon
to demonstrate against the government,
you'll find a gift of five thousand forints
waiting for you. You can claim it in our mobile office.
Today we're not paying extra for enthusiasm,
only for whistling.
Don't bring your own whistle.

We have plenty of first-class merchandise
of proven quality in stock.
(It passed the test with flying colors
in France in Andropov's time.)
It will be distributed this morning free of charge.
Fascination!

Society is not a tray where you can dump your ash,
ash and trash—Cendrars* was of the same opinion while
traveling in Russia. The brain-dead
and those with a cold heart always let others lead them.
Resistance and protests are great gifts of fate.
(Is it a wonder that in the course of history
so many have lined up for it?
For good things you have to line up and wait!)
Vita brevis!
Let a new dawn rip!
Penetration!

A bad mood can poison so many things.
It can poison your health, your spirit,
its toxins soak into the network
of your sentiments.
How much better in the shade of trees!
("Don't you worry while I'm your guide!" says Virgil.)
Justice with a Janus face, where are you now?
Aren't you concerned about misinterpretation?
Misinterpretation is also part of the style.
It has a Leopold Bloom,
knee socks, feverish dreams, a cat,
but not a life.

The powers that be always usurp something—
sometimes the freedom of flight, sometimes confidence.

We're standing blindfolded at the edge of a deep chasm.
From behind we hear the cry: Stop! Not another step!
From the other side: Step forward! Go!

*Blaise Cendrars (1887–1961), Swiss-French poet and novelist, who traveled widely.

KODÁLY CIRCLE IS IN THE PHOTO

(A Körönd is a fénykép része)

> *In memory of the fallen heroes of the 1956 Hungarian
> Uprising.*

The spot of blood shines among the clouds,
neon streetlights sprinkle lazy gleam on your hair.
Kodály Circle is also part of the photo, small
pyres sit around its center. That is where

a door leads to the bundles of fleeting fog;
behind the evening veil old musings quake.
Tumbling walls of scents cover you over.
Under dry bushes fearful winds lie awake.

Time lets out a cry, it dashes off barefoot
from the flames of October; undefeated men.
Once, red stars were falling there with soot.

Your words can now open windows, and one stem
of a rose is a holy icon. The present's live reality
should be dressed in the heavy mantle of memory.

IN THE RED SQUARE OF MOSCOW

(Moszkvában a Vörös Téren)

in the past few days something kept me frightened
yet nothing's happened
the song comes to settle down beside me
from distant regions from brutal winters
from hopeless springs
the soul arrives half-baked
peers into my window
maybe I should open the gates
of sleeping city squares and secrets
should invite someone for an afternoon walk
in Red Square where Pugachev's*
restless soul is organizing
another revolution

this is the new order
the nest of eternal ideologies is empty
the people now split into three camps
waiting for a better dawn
when they look up at the sky
and see through the oligarchy

money is the global seat of power
it has a reproductive organ
its virtue is the holy hope
of demise and creation
change
but what awaits someone who's always waited in vain?

the certainty of being there
the ringing of Easter bells

the comforting angel of prayers

the mandala ideal of battlefields

the orphan feeling of the bird on a twig

the swan neck of unflagging desire

capillaries cleaned by thoughts

the waterfall of muteness

the accelerating light on a twig

the Caucasian rainstorm in cloudless parts

the quiet servant of the inner self

*Yemelyan Ivanovich Pugachev (1742–1775), a pretender to the
Russian throne, who led a great popular insurrection during
the reign of Catherine II. Alexander Pushkin recounted the story
of the rebellion in his *The History of Pugachev* and used some of
the events in his novel *The Captain's Daughter* (1836).

WHAT PHAIDROS FORGOT TO ASK SOCRATES
(Amit Phaidrosz nem kérdezett meg Szokratésztől)

Is writing for real
or the ship of memory gliding
on the waves of time?
Does the written word relieve the mind
of the burden of forgetting?
Is it a crutch with which
to immortalize
what time and space
failed to save?
Does it seduce the writer
with the promise of immortality
to set human events into words,
plowing paper with a pen to
record what he knows or thinks he knows?
Are his words a reflection
of what *was*
and what *is*?
Can he record every move,
every mood,
color and scent
of the *was* and the *is*,
the flash between two rhymes?

THE MORPHEMES OF THOUGHT
(A gondolat morfémái)

We're creations of unquenchable desire.
If we deny the fear lurking inside us,
the disease will break out on our yellowing skin.

Sparrows carry time in their beaks
and sprinkle it in the nest under construction.

Don't you worry, they're already building the unbuildable!
Our souls suck up the Lord's blessing.
They're building peace around us,
the walls of the history not yet in history books,
not even in the news.

Literature is silent now.
(Words are no longer within its reach
as some people believe.)
Togetherness and struggle
have been rooted out from
the flowerbeds of consciousness.

The snare systems, too,
work according to new laws;
immobility
drags anyone down who
always and ardently wants to confess.

(Is there no longer anything to confess?)

It's no use for the monomaniacal willpower
to seek the poison in the flesh of reality.
What is there to find when poisons
of all kinds make up our world?

RIVOLTA CONTRO IL MONDO*
(Rivolta Contro il Mondo)

Go ahead, Caliban, burn the books!
From letters fertile smoke and cinder will rise.
The Lord will remember all with great pretense of concern.
For that you don't have to descend into the underworld.
(Inspiration steadily works at its own survival
fueled by the mystery of reality.)

Rivolta contro il mondo,

> *blaring its astral horn,*
> *I'm undecided, my Lord,*
> *let my spirit get reborn.*

The nothing is a real burden. Creativity, the work: tyranny,
as if it seems harder and harder for us simply to be.

Banish all forms of utopia!
What we do not undertake will persist
under the bell jars of imagination.
Is that preservation? Or self-preservation?
Those who deny knowing you deny existence.

The hunger for the universe sweeps you along.

The hunger for words.
The soul is underfed.
By tomorrow it'll come back to life, purified.
You believe its pulse, its fire, its delirium,
a street of rundown houses side by side.

Why does someone who's been
led down the garden path
want to do the same to you?
Looks at you through fog,
bemused by you.

* Revolt against the world (Italian)

DE OMNI RE SCIBILI*

(De Omni Re Scibili)

The initial second of the new year
dives into soft waves.
I'm sitting on the beach, almost in water,
in conversation about trivia
with the palms leaning over me.
They pay close attention and
in the wind from the Caribbean Sea
they keep nodding
to the things I reveal about myself.
In exchange I learn from one of them
they understand eternity because
they incessantly adore the watery mirror
dropping off at the horizon,
that's their only task, their only passion,
that's how they satiate their desire
for understanding.
"The more steadily we stare at nothing,
the clearer the meaning of our existence
becomes," says another.
"We don't despair if our palm tree life
suddenly sinks into nothingness."
"Neither does it bother us if we learn very little
about the outside world in this short time.
Our failures, the defeat of our thinking, are things
we attribute to our impatience, changeability,
weak determination and our fear of
empty space," adds the third
in the initial seconds of the new year,
while further down the beach the last petard
plunges from the infinity of the sky.

*Of all things knowable (Latin)

NEVER-ENDING LOVEMAKING

(Soha véget nem érő szeretkezés)

unreliable corruption disgusts me

it gets me drunk, stupid and poor

let corruption be brave and original

let it awaken noble thoughts

let it show the power of imagination

let it be like a firestorm

let it destroy everything

and let everything be rebuilt

again and again

let it be the focal point of positive forces

let nothing oppose it

(justice is an intellectual rather than an impulsive act)

let corruption be impetuous, enthusiastic, urbane

let it make the republic flourish

neglecting reason, indifference and dreams

let it be sparklingly blinding

a sweeping force

like a river from a flooding South American source

aphoristically revealing yet indiscreet

Delilah must not break Samson's strength

lift the ban on Cicero's writings

let there be unending pleasure

never-ending lovemaking

let Eros be the shop window

of splendiferous spectacles

a ruthless desire on the threshold of pondering

a fertile desert

a predator plant

for broiling reality is the opposite of tyranny
total historical mistake
that'll remind you of Tacitus, Aristotle,
Rome, Jerusalem, the history of all ages
let it love Machiavelli and exciting perversity
let it adore Kant's logic let it never wilt
let corruption be sentimentally captivating
among the divisive the most vulgarly divisive
the beast of beasts
the hunter of neutrality
a sure way to knock the world off its foundation
(who enjoys standing around, lost in a strange city?)

THE CONSCIENCE OF TREES
(A fák lelkiismerete)

you must appeal to the conscience of trees
their calm is the sign of confidence
that you've coveted for ages
even with a budding mind

their calm is doubt
the probability of the probable
the omnivorous self of
the world with messy hair
now turning silver

trees do not fear failure
rebellion
the cinder of time sifting
into nothingness

trees can see mortals
see our sins
see
what consumes us
that's why trees cling to the sky
with their branches high above

THE DUST
OF MY
EXISTENCE

FOOTPRINT

(Lábnyom)

My poem is a passing footprint
in the soft sands of your soul;
a dream poured by a frisky dawn
through a mute sieve under its control.

Morning is milk and dunked in it
your body explicates the scene,
the past can only torture you until
its tongue grows tired of being mean.

Complaining leaves my reason blurred,
a poison flower is my hope,
just a sliver of this world.

I speak of this need with which I live
while the wispy sunrise silently
pours a new dream through the sieve.

HUGE YELLOW FAIRY TALES

(Nagy sárga meséket)

I'm rounding up a herd of nerves,
huge yellow tales: my childhood,
the cadet keeps running
with a howling olive-branch flag in his hand
and playing with an air gun near my heart.

The anxious two-year-old
creates a smile oasis
like a freshly opened gift package
and defeats the huge yellow fairy tales:
he confiscates my childhood,
my toy horsewhip
and, shrugging his shoulders,

he whacks my nerves into docile
domestic stock.

AT LAST
(Végre)

It's a must to dream,
to make plans,
to create;
and so is to decipher
from the stone prints of sunshine
passion,
impulses,
shadows,
the bodies of trees fallen
into the arms of winds,
houses emerging from distant fog,
the sap of oases,
and to adoringly love,
to adoringly love,
at last
adoringly love
a woman,
the homeland,
God.

I live
with the soul
bandaged,
my blood
seeps through
when I think
about it:
I live.
I LIVE

SEASIDE MORNING WITH HEIDEGGER

(Tengerparti reggel Heideggerrel)

To the memory of Sándor Kilin

Make a ruckus to roust the morning

let the heart of the sea skip a beat,

nudge the Sun to give you

more room

(temporary structure next to a structure).

Words inscribed,

suspension bridges connecting beaches.

Their meaning is lit up by your smile.

A leaf loses its balance,

drops below,

time-space continuum watches it land.

That's all we are: wrinkles in infinity.

No shields to protect us!

NECESSITY
(Necessitas)

no I'm not mumbling
why should I
this morning I diced all my fears
now a peppermint-flavored dawn is
splitting open under your breast
your sigh crashes
into the sigh of the sea
I take with me the sky's blank face
would that I could
preserve this moment
my hope
blooming in your heart

UNCLE SPACE WAVES

(Tér bácsi integet)

The ground and I lie together at rest,
a wheat sheaf bends over me,
summer's light blade penetrates my heart
rhythmically nodding its snowy head.

A skyful of blue descends on me
coloring my blood,
I'm sniffing August winds, a lungful of time,
I feel my summer hopes in my throat,
on my lips the hand of heat,
the cloud host of whispered words
as they flap over my eyes.

Like a thirsty bird I tip my head
sipping my silence,
my hand starts to fly off in farewell,
Uncle Space waves to me.

BREATHING TERRAINS

(Lélegző tájak)

Ever notice?—
in the sod of the body an earthly dream is at work,
and every time you live through the whisperings
of a vitreous winter's idle trees
or the caresses of summer's bayonets,
you feel love
swell into a river
and flood the breathing terrains of your land,
and the seed sown earlier
springs up as a live wheat sheaf
in the lap of brightly rocking dawns.

MORNING IN BARBADOS

(Barbadosi reggel)

A set of thoughts strung on a string
shaking around the necks of palm trees.
Time crumbled existence into small pieces,
the faces of patient flowers filter the light.
Pillars of moist air rise from the sea
toward a dispersing sky.
A wind scrapes the nude bodies of waves,
on the birdfeeder a hummingbird finds a home.
In the sand a live god begins to roam.

THE FABRIC
(A szövet)

It's some fabric I purchased,
made of unreality,
it's easy
to measure and
take to the tailor
who tilts his head
with reservation,
he keeps fingering it;
let's see
what it's made of,
how fine the texture is,
how free it is of small faults
that an expert like him
can easily find by touch;
then suddenly he clutches
the heart of the fabric,
let's see how easily
it wrinkles
or how well it can ignore
the tailor's rude test
and relax to its smooth state.
Finally,
holding his head high
the tailor gives his verdict,
yes, a suit can be sewn using this fabric,
but where is the man who will wear it?

SMILEY FACE
(Happy Face)

Road signs and direction

at the junctions of life:

exit this way,

no exit there,

this way to hell

that way to heaven.

One has purpose,

the other has depth.

One is transparent,

the other cryptic.

They belong to the genre of the impossible.

Like pre-arranged questions,

silenced answers,

a worldview,

an opinion dancing on the edge of a blade.

Above a chasm, only

ideals survive,

well-balanced convictions

with dedication and direction

that hold them together.

The form letter is blind.

In spite of the happy face emoji

clicked

onto the bottom of the sheet.

SPEAR-FISHERMEN

(Halászok)

day after day I watch
the men fishing in the sea
I feel like joining them
I envy their weightlessness
and the weightiness of their lives
every move they make
the way they dive into the unknown

BALLAD OF PAIN
(Ballada a fájdalomról)

His parents divorced.
He was not quite eight yet.
He spoke about his pain to everyone;
the neighbors, his schoolmates,
his grandparents far off in a village
and at the lakeside to the fish swimming in the water.
He related the event with such a heart-wrenching affect
every time and to everyone
that often he began to feel
there was no one in the world
who could speak of pain
as tragically and convincingly.
As fate would have it, he eventually made a career of it.
He had daily engagements, with good pay,
to give talks on pain, to dramatize the impalpable,
the soul-killing flames of pain.
He was already living in retirement, alone, in seclusion,
when a pretty young lady asked him to give one more
performance as the world expert on the subject of pain.
He could not resist the chance to make a comeback,
but then he spent many a sleepless night trying to
reconstruct his show,
what, when and how to say,
and in what order to ratchet up the tension of the story
he had so successfully told all through his life.
On his appearance he was greeted with stormy applause.
He got a standing ovation and bouquets tossed at him.
Then the audience quieted down,
everyone awaiting his words with bated breath.
He stepped up to the podium, his back erect like a pine.
But no sound left his lips, neither then, nor ever again.

BLACK SEAGULL

(Fekete sirály)

I carry you with me to me
an alien coffin without a hearse
I carry you as far as I can see
to keep you from fire or curse
I carry you across state borders
in my hands and on my shoulders

in cloudbursts you are my cross
my sin and verse predicting loss
dark doubts in a bleak terrain
I want to order it to stop the pain
and on your skin a tender spring
that melting iceberg words can bring

I carry you far but I can't remain
you are on fire and far in vain
digging a hole and setting a snare
your devil's heart without a care
for it though I'd lie down on the rack
but racks now torture by their lack

BRUISED BIRD

(Zúzott madár)

I had too much to drink again,

I got stinking drunk by evening,

in dim light spiders,

gray lizards are spying.

On the hill they're burning

the fallen leaves,

a year of drought.

Lights turning silent

over unharnessed terrain.

If they flare up again,

I will not envy them.

From a palm tree Byron is laughing,

perched on a branch Goethe

sticks out a tongue,

his shadow swept by winds.

The sky looks angry,

makes me stumble,

but I keep lugging

your burden

in my sulking heart.

A bruised bird is thrashing inside me,

slapping black piano keys.

One raised finger stops it.

Pests are chewing time,

a cactus flower in the garden winks at me.

MORNING IN SAN FRANCISCO

(San Franciscó-i reggel)

Let your mind revisit that day,
pour the light of the Acropolis into a secret,
rattle the chassis of time,
let the reverie offspring escape your touch,
let young fog tremble at the sight of your muscles.

Morning is a crimson train.
It runs away from your steps,
fleeting in fear
you might trample over it;
your worldview and mood are—
confidentially—hungover.
The purple of the Golden Gates
dissolves its steel cells in the sea,
cuts into the flesh of boredom with a mast
piercing the gray clouds.

The area is undressing.
Wherever you look,
automobiles
among well-dressed homes,
metallic fish tossed ashore,
glistening spring roams.
On the sidewalk, just a step away,
a sweeping wind is on the job.

Back in the hotel,
under cool arcades,

a soft monologue on the lips of guests,
a child shuffling his feet before the lift.
Sesame opens,
the neon snake gives a light burst,
it feels different here:
balled-up cotton shirt.

The peace has tremors in the halls,
historic black-and-white
photos on the walls,
the horrors of nature,
houses collapsed into pain,
nineteen hundred and six,
one look quakes the ground again.

Stepping into the room
you look for the key to the future,
yesterday it was still there,
in the pocket of the jacket draped over the chair,
the ship sunk in mystical fog unseen,
submerged in a vision,
a stray submarine.

CATHEDRAL OF ETERNAL WINTER

(Katedrális az örök télnek)

At the age of sixteen I had no
intention of saving the world, but I
did fancy a revolution, the kind that
lets a person freak out. (No one can expect
any less fantasizing from a youngster
with incipient fuzz on his chin.)
Besides, the thrill of revolution was the most
obvious choice for someone born in the city
of the thirteen martyrs,* he didn't
have to borrow ideas from outsiders;
being attached to the iron vertebrae of the locale,
the environment and the history meant for you
to measure up to the forebears and to follow their
example, even unto hallowed death. Damjanich,
Pöltenberg, Knézic would've agreed.
Except they may have added softly:
"My boy, there must be a better way
of going about this."
Did I expect this cautionary note?
Did it mean anything to me at that time?
I can't tell now, but I do say even a solo
revolution is useless; actually, abhorrent.
What remains is the word, the true word to be posted
on the sacred banner, kindling a world conflagration,
not a hundred times but a hundred thousand times.
No challenge is more honorable than to dedicate
oneself to the eternal struggle, and yet one has

to get the firewood ready every morning and,
while wielding the axe, think about the future.

The concrete walls of the future allow little room
for someone determined to break out.
Anyone eager to jettison all burdens
should bury his head in the sand
where there's nothing to worry about
inside or out.
In any case, destiny calls for a hard winter,
and in there he should dig a tunnel with defiance
if he wants to make his denial undeniable,
and his investment pay off.
The withered hand looks good in this area,
no one is hurt by the lack of recognition,
by the minute lost after others are gone,
by the roller-coaster ride, seasons upside down,
by how easily every night gets
untangled inside.

You get lots of help feeling cold.
Although, unforgettable are world-saving schemes.
Pushing chairs aside they seem to stand here as dreams.
The rest is superficial spat.
The universe can hardly ever be seen,
breath speeds up, defeat gets easier,
stuck in the mud, who can remember
how it happened, whatever did.
A new suit steps out of the closet,
a wondrous change, who needs old roots,
they only wither under new boots.

The spirit hunts for dodgers,
sincerity is worth nothing today;
an archaeological find
in my room on special display.

So many gifts in this luxury
and so many words misunderstood!
Attention strays following a broken line,
thought gets derailed from its focal point,
and tomorrow it'll go without notice
if someone gets locked out.
The fate of little fish lacks in tragedy,
it's only a minor detail in the great scheme of things.
Fear is conceived in a night concentrate,
veiled in fog it grows really great,
so much so that I tend to disregard
whose words I'm supposed to guard.
Autumns and I are in a running race.
At the starting line they all got ready,
then it was my turn to kneel at my place.

So much about running amok.
The days were anemic and pale,
the nights tubercular,
starvation salted by silence,
the roadside trees stuttered
a drunken diatribe.
Planes looked like cranes to me,
I wanted them to give me a ride.

By the lakeside
scurries a light

a mute equation
my pain ration

every activity
soon imprisoned me

They put a shine
on the tabletop,
but who can recall that,
the tide of time has washed away
the chair, the hat,
ever since
we have shame to endure
with some nostalgia
mixed in
with us for cure,
the story trembles with us
with steel signals
on its uniform.

General Görgey** rolls
our future tolls.

The homeland is no more,
mute is now the battle roar,
honor is all that stays
with thick snowfalls since those days.

The Hungarian soul bathing in eternal winter,
I can see you and wish you the best,
though sharpened knives in my heart
live on without a minute's rest,

I'm the builder of the cathedral to eternal winter,

I have to hide my treasures in icy cold,

my voice, my handshake, my face are not for me to hold,

clinging to the long hair of time in vain

even if I swallow the noise;

acceptance offers nothing to gain,

waiting for better days is not for me.

I leave the cathedral of winter to posterity.

*The Hungarian Revolution against the Austrian monarchy, which started on March 15th of 1848 and ended in defeat in 1849, remains a determinative event in Hungarian history, a pivotal aspect of the national identity. The nation fought for civil rights, social reforms and independence from the Austrian Empire ruled by the Habsburg Dynasty. In the end, only the joint army of Russian and Austrian forces could defeat the Hungarians. Following the defeat, thirteen Hungarian generals: Lajos Aulich, János Damjanich, Károly Knézic, György Lanner, Károly Leiningen-Westerburg, József Nagysándor, Ernő Pöltenberg, Ignác Török, Károly Vécsey were executed by hanging in Arad on October 6, 1849; Arisztid Dessewffy, Vilmos Lázár, Ernő Kiss, József Schweidel were shot in the head because of their friendship with the Prince of Luxembourg. Hanging was deemed a humiliation. On the same day, Count Lajos Batthány, the first Hungarian prime minister, was executed in Pest at an Austrian military garrison.

**Artúr Görgey (1818–1916) was a Hungarian general of the 1848–49 War of Independence, whose military talents have always been tarnished by accusations that he betrayed the cause. Immediately following the struggle, Görgey was branded a traitor by the Hungarian president, Lajos Kossuth, who referred to him as "Hungary's Judas." Kossuth alleged that Görgey had undermined the fragile revolutionary government by surrendering to the Russians at Világos (today Șiria, Romania), and delivered his officers and soldiers to Austrian vengeance while he secured amnesty and payment for himself. Unfortunately for Görgey, these perceptions have continued to be a focus of debate in Hungarian historiography.

VISIT TO THE OLD COLLEGE TOWN

(Majorana Kolozsvárra látogat)

Today I could not dig any deeper,
in the corner café some memory yawns,
the leaping tower of the citadel beckons
to me, a stranger, inviting me for a cognac,
but it fails to entice me, a set of tired
seagull wings lies before me on the table.

A double entendre can fling you past land's geometry,
handing you a bouquet of adventures,
adventures I could have lived through,
but fate did not have me in mind;
with holes in my shoes I roamed the streets
of Kolozsvár holding hands with the wind.
That child then lacked enthusiasm,
the Calvary of hope, the magic-studded
mirage of distant destinations.
Loneliness and rage were spinning before me,
playing a duet, boarding up blind windows.

One can put up with want,
even wear it proudly like a Sunday white shirt,
boasting with it as with a bit of Virgil-style wisdom,
but hunger is not easy to banish from one's thoughts
thus abstract it while it keeps returning with the meteorites
of reality, pounding the man ever harder whose
privilege is doing penance.

The Golgotha of thought is quite populous,
space is ever expanding,

the Szamos banks cast a crazy shadow
on the freezing nothing.
Shakespeare could've walked in peace like that,
far from London, from everyday cares,
and yet close enough to the things we
must play, say, feel and lie about every day.

Theater was really theater back then, too,
and light-soaked willows of the riverbank
and time reddened on the branches of the soul;
the mystery kept growing in the body of
untold legends as did unused stones, the feeling
of collapse, and the haughty power of oceans—that
I've traveled ever since.

Every night now here and there
I sit on the grassy riverbank
as a cricket
singing among drowsy stars.

EMPTY TRAINS

(Üres vonatok)

The mornings depart,

and they arrive without you.

Empty trains.

Your spirit flashes now and then

on the hem of a sky foundering in light.

Sentences fog the steep slopes

of long-gone lands,

staring into nothing,

fatigued by now.

Acacia trees have again invaded the riverbank,

the injured in the autumn storm are

cared for by tender new winds.

Last night the neighbor

was not drilling through the wall,

in the abandoned room the bed is empty,

the place of lovemaking is open,

the painted wooden pillow is cold but still

buzzed by an antique dream as before;

joy would like to sneak back, but there's

no one to ferry it to the other shore.

DE ARTIS POETICAE NATURA

(De Artis Poeticae Natura)

The poetry of things approaches infinity,

I hear the lakeside willow's simpering.

Although the soul can help you through the winter,

acacia buds are opened by the force of spring.

A wordlessly festooned plaza for me is there,

the sounds of holiday psalms encrust the air.

Yet no one will go to hell for me.

When I get into its stream, the lyrical craze

trusses my body, its spirit ablaze.

It glues up the hair of night-wrapped pines,

and by morning it bursts into heavenly tears.

Dipped in my blood its magic steel pen consigns

me to the legends of mute balladeers.

GOD NEVER WROTE TO A MORTAL AS TOUCHINGLY
(Halandónak Isten nem írt soha ilyen meghatóan)

Sunshine copies a text on my desk.

Every day and on purpose,

to see if I can unravel the words.

God never wrote a letter of such gravity to a mortal.

Exorcism is not expected of me,

I'm supposed to be the way I was

created: curious and diligent.

Earthly treasures are out,

I am to seek the meaning of life in the arts.

(Loving poetic lines, I am the slavish lover of love!)

Avoid fear!

Fear is not good for my mental and moral health.

I'm to be like a volcano

and eject good and bad into the sky,

I'm to get purified and thus empowered to purify.

But I was not asked to account for my faith.

And what for?

Those who believe will end up crucified.

ANOTHER KIND OF SUMMER
(Másféle nyár)

This poem is an instrument.
I have it on rental for only a minute,
hoping to affect your consciousness.
My plan is based on the Trojan horse;
I'll steal myself into your thoughts.
I want you to like the cloud
stranded over you, daydream about
past summers, be confident
and in good cheer.
Following this script, you can affect me,
yes, me who rented this poem
in order to steal myself into your thoughts,
fix up a sloppy, emotional sentence of yours,
spy with a curious look on the indecision
skulking under the horizon,
give up my doubts;
if I run into a mild breeze
on shadowy Rákóczi Street in Budapest
while I feel how pleasant it is to take
a stroll in this poem
without any care or commitment
and to pass this sensation on to you.
Please, take it in your hand,
listen for the soft heartbeat of this summer in it,
drink up its scent.

SYMMETRY

(Szimmetria)

the sea entraps me on its tongue
stirring tired breezes' song
freely bleeds a mighty crest
on my heart in iced arrest

the fiery sun flaunts its shine
for whom and to what design
on the backs of beams I stroll
stains are burning on my soul

stirring tired breezes' song
the sea entraps me on its tongue
stains are burning on my soul
on the backs of beams I stroll

for whom and to what design
the fiery sun flaunts its shine
on my heart in iced arrest
freely bleeds a mighty crest

GLEAM SLIVER

(Fényszilánk)

A horde of butterflies taking off.

For a moment of truth a breath is enough.

Overused molds. Maybe sins.

On its see-through spots, fever begins.

Its sac is damp and melts like tulle.

The fragrant glaze holds on to the morning shine.

No joke, no confession coerced.

No boundaries.

The silence and passion are so many quarries

but there's no one to share them with you.

On a flimsy twig a wee little bird.

Its beak opens and closes, its eyes slivers of gleam.

It takes off but where to?

The brash century takes a seat

and shuts your mouth for you.

THE DUST OF MY EXISTENCE

(Létem pora)

A void inside me urges me on to great things;

I've become a crow's nest of zealous words.

Weakness holds out the fulfillment of strength.

It halts. It comes to life in creative works.

The void is fertile. I've seen huge fires die,

the lava of volcanoes come to belly-crawl.

Light is hungry, straw flame, an icon, deity.

There's a spirit of *self* in invisible loyalty.

Emptiness is all, it raised me as I am,

the time on my knees is Scythian.

Prodigal nonexistence is eyeing me,

I'm a dispersed cloud, failure and success;

my guard is the iron hand of nothingness.

The dust of my existence washed out to sea.

SEVEN BIRDS
(Hét madár)

My life is an empty hole.
Blackberries wither on the vine.
When my sigh begins to fly,
seven birds escort it in a line.
They watch the frost erect a nest
of my heart in house arrest.

IT'S SNOWING IN THE BOWER

(A lugasban hull a hó)

Sitting in a bower,

With the hand of silence

Squeezing my throat.

The moment is a squirrel,

Would like to gambol

But can't

Knee-deep in snow.

Sitting in the bower

Like someone left

In the garden by solitude

After the lights went on.

Would like to go inside

But can't

Knee-deep in snow.

LEARNING TO FLY

(Majorana repülni tanul)

nothing but zipping joy, the doubt,
the monotonous rattle of the revved-up
engine, the canvas weightlessness
of the flight, the floating of a jay,
the sensation of a sudden getaway,
the kill-excitement of getting detached,
the flushed mortal soul inside,
the experience of unexpected flight,
there's neither land nor sky under you,
in the abyss a patch of earth below
and above a handful of blue
that you can no longer tell apart if you try,
the moment-land from the moment-sky

THE WIND

(A szél)

Asks me if I lied,
then bored, pushes me aside,
a lonesome moon lights up the sky.
I watch it motionless,
it wounds me, I confess,
it melts gold glint in the waters of my eye.

No soul can persevere,
I no longer fear
what can make the fainthearted perspire.
Small cloud forts grow
with houses below,
and then tired thoughts set them on fire.

Mortality sprints.
Rips into slings
under bushes rattled by a scare.
Egos are told
like tinkling gold,
on the cobblestones a shadow hunts for air.

I hurry off the curb.
Waiting for a word,
for a lighter homebound load to bring.
Got no friend of note,
nor an overcoat,
and the evening's hair flutters in the wind.

CONNECTING

(Kapcsolva)

Europe reporting

a point made in a dozen languages

Louis XVI likes to go bowling

Mozart is taking music lessons

the trial in the case of Josef K is in progress

Joyce is stealing glimpses of himself in the mirror

Déry* is counting unfinished sentences

order still prevails

all's quiet on the Western Front

Europe still lacks

the latest nuclear weapons

* Tibor Déry (1894–1977) was a Hungarian writer, sometimes at
odds with the ruling Communist Party.

NINE OCTAVES

(Kilenc Oktáv)

On a ragged soul the embers of words remain,
On trite roads the trite magic of marching hordes;
On reality's flimsy canvas it's cocaine.

The lap of winds nurtures sheets of rotting sails,
On the fiery prayer-mound of imagination
The ritual of torturous visions flails.

Thought overheats, its dense branches soar
With lights and glints for the séance of willpower.
Nine octaves are buried in their music score.

No escape; dead are those who had their say.
Wild winters scatter their handful of dust,
Gone forever are the debtors of the day.

On the slopes of love a naked mountain peak;
Let the merchants of dreams spy on you
In desert lands, undefended and bleak.

The mouth casts about for a word in the sky;
Today's Croesus is clothed in oblivion,
Only tomorrow knows what today will signify.

Icy sparks ignite an inferno so sublime.
The people celebrate a new Prometheus,
Recording his painful cries on the skin of time.

The air is abuzz, a naked prey to flames,
It'll be the world, and the word will be hostage
To one once maimed by fever in Hera's name.

Pointing at the mountain, quoting God and good,
Hoping to relive every sensation of the past,
Go, launch a new boat, or wish you could.

But do it, and also understand the rhyme
That strings together the chain of millennia;
Thus to get aborted from the womb of time.

Impossible. And yet it never lets me lag,
But chases me with temptations, stitching
An ancient emblem to our silken flag.

A ghost emerges from the mist of sly
Suspicions by the order of things.
Fear, the aging shepherd, wanders by.

The faith-blade of rebellious fantasies,
And in you the earthly copy of a rigid sky,
The nightmare distilled by summer bliss.

The friend of a wind left on a blond shore,
Impossible to retrieve by now, its memory
Is to be buried deep inside the spirit's core.

You're still capable of creating a need,
And fall upon the past with knives and words,
A dead twig reeling in a visionary creed.

Sunshine glows inside you, set to hug you there.
Would rather fly, tenderness gleams on its feathers;
What is there to see, wounded, coming up for air?

On a ragged soul the embers of words remain,
On trite roads the trite magic of marching hordes;
On reality's flimsy canvas it's cocaine.

TAKING ASHES UP THE HILL

(Hamut viszek a hegyre)

Crestfallen flashes of light; you're away.
You worry me and what the whirls will say.

I'm taking ashes up the hill on my back.
Biscuits, baked in ashes, also in the pack.

Life's a glittering, cool, amazing thing,
hope sways in the wind; God is reveling.

By the time I reach the blinding crest
my life is no life, of little interest.

INVENTORY

(Leltár)

"The inventory's done." Nothing more. Whitewashed wall.
Croupier in ceaseless winter. Stake piled on stake.
Two crickets fiddling. That's all.

The kettle's empty in the kitchen. Suppers incinerate.
Book, booze, nothing doing, blue skunk-cabbage, blue.
Muddy city gate.

My freshly pressed shirt. Give it to you off my back.
I'll put them to sleep, should doubts attack.
You're true stuff. Nothing. Just enough.

THE MIRAGE OF OUR FATE

THE MIRAGE OF OUR FATE
(Sorsunk délibábja)

My Prince, the poets have all departed!
Their fading footprints can still be read
In labyrinths of light. They did not cheat,
But simply got tired of the Quintus bed,
Rome is no longer glorified by their songs.
These poets are for us to celebrate,
To deck their brows with laurel wreaths.
Their stray souls paint the mirage of our fate.

And yet they could've continued in
The timeless melancholy of Halcyon
Where the searing fire of roses burns
And wise inspirations carry on,
Weaving new fables, *mutato nomine*
*de te fabula narratur** fills the slate,
the news before us, whatever for?
Their stray souls paint the mirage of our fate.

Even Rome no longer needed their song,
*Ridentem dicere verum quid vetat,***
Common sense gets drunk on truth,
New pen is not *donatur* by their lot.
What is missing in this new solitude
Among the busy stars is hot debate,
And not the opiate recited by poets.
Their stray souls the mirage of our fate.

Moral

When the flames inside again turn free
They'll bring back the age of poetry.
Steer to get the wind behind your sails:
In joy the mirage of our fate prevails.

* *Change the name, and the story is told about you.* (Latin quote by Quintus
  Horatius Flaccus or Horace)
** *What is to prevent one from telling the truth as he laughs?* (Latin quote by
  the same poet)

FRANCESCO PETRARCA

(Francesco Petrarca)

I'm not at home in the hills of Arqua,
Here, like everywhere, I'm a foreigner.
My father sent me to study law but it's
Reading Cicero and Virgil I prefer.

The landscape fills my heart with glow,
Devils and angels keep haunting me.
I survived Florence and Avignon,
To the sonnet though I can't claim paternity.

As someone well-versed in prosody,
I hold Latin syllables under my tongue,
Laura's eyes are my constant company,

Where the people are neither old nor young.
Ulysses' fate follows my fate wherever I go,
In the unclouded sky of Padva I'm to glow.

A WALK BY THE ARNO RIVER

(Séta az Arno partján)

> *In the 1504th year of the Lord, three Italian artists lived in Florence: Leonardo da Vinci, Michelangelo Buonarroti and Rafaello Sanzio; Sandro Botticelli lived in a nearby village but often visited the city.*

I'm taking a walk along the Arno;

the facades of Florentine houses are reflected in the water,

like a collage of photographs

they bend in the softly ruffled mirror,

paying no attention to me. The river keeps crawling;

rejuvenated by sunshine, it glistens.

I can see Michelangelo, who hurries along

with Urbino, his loyal servant;

perhaps his mind is on a new sonnet

he's to bring his love, Tommaso dei Cavalieri,

in fiery, passionate lines,

but the outside world is cruel and desolate.

Dark shadows fall on Buonarroti's face,

what the hell are they after in Florence?

the Raffaello and the da Vinci gang? he wonders;

in his imagination the *David* statue, carved from a chunk

of marble, comes alive and meets his gaze.

A southern wind runs along the road,

I stroll hand-in-hand with my thoughts,

my silent shadow follows me,

and I can hear the song of river fish.

Botticelli is approaching on the sidewalk by the riverbank.

He had been summoned to the city to help decide

where to place Michelangelo's *Il Gigante.*
The square near the town hall would be ideal, figures
the fifty-eight-year-old master as the Apelles self-portrait
appears to his inner eye.
A young woman passes him. The face seems familiar; he turns back,
but it's too late to see her features.
When I painted the *Birth of Venus*—he racks his brains—
I was not thinking of Aphrodite, although the shell motif
connected with her body and soul.
And what was the secret behind the fact that only Apelles
was chosen to paint Alexander the Great, and his lover Campaspe
using only four colors:
yellow, crimson, white and black?
And where was the virtue in the act?
Art must serve religion
and nothing else,
on that I agree with Savonarola—

A southern wind runs along the road,
I stroll hand-in-hand with my thoughts,
my silent shadow follows me,
and I can hear the song of river fish.

Beyond the river, on the other side, the terrain
balloons like Venus's breasts. Cedars, olive trees
are chatting softly, covered by thin dew,
the veins of color are butterfly wings.
In the distance a lean voice,
Gian Giacomo Caprotti da Oreno,*
a thief, a cheat, greedy and obstinate,
he entreats da Vinci to let him stop painting under

the alias of Andrea Salai, it's humiliating,

and if the master has any regard for him,

he should make him, Gian, immortal.

Leonardo di ser Pietro da Vinci doesn't answer,

a few days earlier he promised Machiavelli

to work with him on a plan

of diverting the Arno River.

But Salai speaks up again, arguing

and swearing eternal love.

His gesticulating hands are flattened in place by da Vinci,

who looks into his eyes;

upon my death *Mona Lisa* will be yours—he says softly—

and even I can't tell

how many legends and tales that painting will inspire.

I made poor Raffaello worry about it, too,

few are those who understand it, my dear Salai,

just a smile,

yes,

a smile that has puzzled me all my life; I deem

it'll one day surpass the priciest diamond's gleam.

*A much younger man, still better known as *Salai*, who for decades enjoyed the older Leonardo's close friendship.

SPINOZA REDUX

(Spinoza Redux)

If there's no such thing as truth,
we never have to tell what's true.
Doesn't that ease the soul
and liberate man
from the prison of determinism?
Space tightens on the skin of thought,
takes a cast of its form, if it has one, if it has
something that can be called a shape, that is,
an attribute, as Spinoza would say,
Baruch Spinoza, who was excommunicated
by the zealous Jews.

Determinatio negatio est!

How simple! All we have to do is define God,
and then we can forget about everything else,
even things created by God: the substance.
Even ourselves from our selves
and what we think of ourselves,
the thought of thought,
even the diaphanous hint of thought,
the veins rooted in ethereal space,
the vision.
We're floundering in the tangled net of the dilemma.
It's awful the way facts always prevent us
*from getting to know reality.**
Facts always suppress what reality projects
on the tulle-white canvas of existence,
making us lose our way in
the ever-sinking sunsets of our vigils.

*These last two italicized lines are quoted from Rainer Maria Rilke in translation.

ON THE POND OF SPACE
(A tér taván)

> *Sacred poesy is a mute swan,*
> *And silent forever in cold waters.*
> —Dániel Berzsenyi*

Poesy is the glow of exploding stars,

we take in its visions,

Vivaldi's music,

the translucent cupola of sound,

the protective sac, we order clouds to cover it,

bloodless sky.

What ran aground in space

can start a new life in meadows.

The melody defends

the magic seed sown into the ground,

the hotbed of the force working inside it,

and creates a new future,

a magnetic field for a handful of love.

Poesy,

a hint wafting from the ancient world;

Aeolian,

its transparent linen flutters,

saturated with steamy winds.

In the distance fires flare up,

they glide through the dim light

followed by shades like desires pursued.

The fire mingles with the scent of light and grasses.

Eagles are watching what this earthly life nurtures,
and swoop down on it if it dares to move.

Poesy is the white swan of timelessness,
swimming silent on the pond of space.

*Dániel Berzsenyi (1776–1836), the most self-conflicted poet of Hungarian literature. This trait made him a lonesome, introverted and bitter person. His works show influence of Classicism and Romanticism.

RENDEZVOUS

(Randevú)

I stop somewhere, waiting for you. *
Perhaps under a neon streetlamp puffing
light and winking toward the pond,
wanting to light up all things all at once,
like the heart well-fed
with freshly acquired joys
yet keeps grabbing this and that
wanting really to fill up with avid
restlessness.
Fill up, forever.
Fill up with it just for now
and leap over to the crippled moment,
over the gray ditch,
to the willows swaying their heads,
to the dim silence where the tigers of the evening
are shining their eyes and sniffing the scent of blood
through nostrils opened wide; it's not just a hint
of curiosity whipped by hunger that drives them,
the hunting instinct coded into the genes,
but the natural savagery of the fatal bites,
the aerialist and flamboyant cruelty of a predator,
or the flame of an impatient seizure
when it skips into dry hay with yellowish-purple glow;
that's how open jaws snap shut on everything
in their way.
A wind is jogging around me with manly arrogance.
Until you are fully realized,
I stop somewhere, waiting for you.

* Last line (verse 52) of Walt Whitman's poem *Song of Myself.*

ONLY HANDS AND FEET AND HEADS . . .
(Csak kezek, és lábak és fejek...)

I'm translating a poem by Whitman. It's rough going.
I drop it, pick it up again; I linger on the threshold
of meaning. Attention glides over it.
You come to mind, what you promised not long ago,
you were going to recruit someone *(. . . and become undisguised*
and naked, / I am mad for it to be in contact with me.)
and the three of us make love. I unbutton your blouse,
taking my time with it, with nervously shaky fingers, until
your liberated breast falls into my hand, your lips meld
to the mouth of that other woman whom we undress
in slow motion as we all melt in one another's
kisses. *(And what I assume you shall assume, /*
For every atom belonging to me as good
belongs to you.) We hug one another,
dim mood-lighting is rocking us gently in its arms,
caprices and compulsion sear us, fever pounds
in our ears, mountains begin to rise, and on the hills
squatting around us the lawn of the flung-open laps
silently appears. Only hands and feet and heads,
in the veranda of shoulders fiery fingers stroll up and down,
and we dissolve the ink of the night in our drooling saliva
(Echoes, ripples, buzz'd whispers,
love-root, silk-thread, crotch and vine.)
like Lombard silk the skin tightens on the bars of ribs,
the white patches of nudity flash,
arcades grow above sighs,
on its noiseless remains a kiss finds rest.
Three boiling bodies gasping for breath
under the foliage of touching.

*The parts in parentheses are quoted from Walt Whitman's *Song of Myself.*

PASSWORDS TO IMMORTALITY

(Jeligék a halhatatlanságnak)

On the day of Péter Esterházy's burial,* August 2, 2016

Patience is superfluous!

It does not untie the secondary verbs of the heart.

Does not erect a cathedral to sunken words.

The horrified butterflies of the minute flit in every direction,

the terrain is populated with the regiments of mortality.

In a last will & testament there are no question marks;

this is the most amazing part of it! No question marks!

Sentences, yes. But only basic statements with few modifiers.

To be used when knocking on the door of the eternal present.

Surreal.

Let us speak of the total entity.

Totality also contains the thing

that under some pretense got left out.

He has the temerity to collect the parts

while concentrating only on the big picture, doesn't he?

The dream-catcher awakens not only in the morning

but on thoughts slipped into the mantle of fate,

when it's not necessary to write down the unwritten,

to speak about the unspeakable,

to confess that which cannot be confessed.

Does the head hold the church or the other way around?

Transcendence creates a bucolic mood.

It cuts to the marrow of life, it helps you through budding springs,

because we must catch summer.

Summer solves all problems. If we trip, it helps us to our feet,

it heals us, gives us, the hapless, a chance

as a wreath of light woven of hopefulness.

The fires of summer rising as high as that of resurrection.

Trees are resting on the ground by the road to Ganna**
in the shade of handkerchief-size clouds.
Morsels of memories in the grip of imagination.
The wind regains its consciousness, seeing none of us,
it rises and brushes us off its lapel;
as he stands up he slips out of his jacket,
his shirt flutters untucked from the pants.
The only solution is to wait patiently
until the world comes to.
Then there'll be a new start, the dream, creativity.
Mute signals on our Milky Way.
The word has fallen silent in Hunnia.

*Péter Esterházy (1950–2016) was a prominent Hungarian prose writer.
**Ganna is a small village where the ancestral home and the mausoleum of the
Esterházy family are located.

THE CUSTOMS AGENT'S SINGLE FLOWER

(A vámos egyetlen virága)

To the memory of Imre Kertész

With a single flower in his hand*
the eternal customs agent still stands at the border,
waiting for the next scheduled train to arrive.
As usual, the final recognition is again
late in coming,
spring flowers are accumulating in the corner,
memory rummages in the foliage of visions,
das Ding an sich,** an anthropological find,
in Königsberg's legacy,
the logical constant of existence
in the peepholes of the spirit:
the universe manifests itself
only in the midst of its eternal transformation.
Spring flowers accumulate in the corner,
the sun bores its way through the chinks in the shutters.
From now on only the oeuvre can be consistent,
the internal relations no longer count.
We slice across centuries without finding rest
in this restlessness consistently attacking us.
We erect statues to the heroes of Sparta,
and one evening we take a quick look at the Cheops Pyramid
(his actual name was Khnum-Khufu Horus Medjedu,
but you wouldn't know that from the Westcar Papyrus
nor from Herodotus;
not even the Manetho Scrolls tell the real story,
perhaps even back then history was subject to revision),

not only for the view

and the amazing beauty of unbroken space,

but also to get acquainted

with the night stooping over it,

the dark night that

covers us up

at its leisure,

one by one,

as sadness did in our childhood.

*Allusion to *Notebook*, a work by Imre Kertész (1929–2016), the Nobel
 Prize–winning author.

**"The thing-in-itself" or the concept of *noumenon* in Immanuel Kant's
 transcendental analysis, a philosophical approach he initiated and named.

BALLAD OF NEW YORK
(New York-i ballada)

After an old newspaper article

An exceptionally warm and windy autumn morning,
the eleven-year-old Johnny is playing Monopoly with
the seven-year-old Mary on the brick floor of the barn.

With sharp blades the sunshine rends breaches in the picket fence.

A bad roll of the dice lands Johnny
on the Go to Jail square.
Upset, he objects.
Wants to repeat the roll.
Mary insists on the rules,
and when her reasoning gets no result,
she throws a tantrum.
She curses out Johnny something awful, and
he stabs her in the chest with a pitchfork.

With sharp blades the sunshine rends breaches in the picket fence.

The Welsh poet Dylan Thomas tosses the eighteenth
shot of whiskey down his throat
and staggers out from the White Horse Tavern of Greenwich Village,
but after a few steps he collapses.
Two friends help him up and take him to the Chelsea Hotel.
Next day in St. Francis Hospital the poet
departs from this world.

With sharp blades the sunshine rends breaches in the picket fence.

Johnny takes the saw off the rotting wall of the barn.

He cuts Mary's body into pieces.
He places each piece in a black garbage bag
with a good-sized stone from the garden,
and throws the bags into the Hudson.

With sharp blades the sunshine rends breaches in the picket fence.

The White Horse Tavern can be found
at 567 Hudson Street in New York City,
between 11th and Perry Streets.
The visitor can see a painting of a white horse
next to a portrait of Dylan Thomas on the wall,
and he can learn from the bartender that
Norman Mailer, Allen Ginsberg, Jack Kerouac,
John Ashbery and Frank O'Hara used to be regulars.

With sharp blades the sunshine rends breaches in the picket fence.

A late autumn rainy day
Johnny plays Monopoly
in the barn with Max, who's
wandered in from the street.
An unlucky roll of the dice lands
Johnny on the Go to Jail square.
He wants to re-do the roll.
Max hotly protests.
Johnny stabs him in the chest with a pitchfork.
He cuts the body into pieces with a saw
and puts them into black plastic bags
with a stone in each
from the garden.

He throws the packages in the Hudson.

With sharp blades the sunshine rends breaches in the picket fence.

The White Horse Tavern in Greenwich Village is empty.
There's a sign on the entrance door:
Closed on account of illness!

With sharp blades the sunshine rends breaches in the picket fence.

Johnny feels lonely. He's been skipping school for days.
Roaming the streets he runs into some boys he knows.
Loudly, trying to outdo one another,
they start boasting of their pranks.
Johnny too comes out with what he did to Mary and Max.

With sharp blades the sunshine rends breaches in the picket fence.

Deep-sea divers are searching the Hudson River.

Shall I unbolt or stay
Alone till the day I die
Unseen by stranger-eyes
In this white house?
Hands, hold you poison or grapes?*

*From "Ears in the Turrets Hear" by Dylan Thomas (1914–1953).

WAKING MÁRAI
(Márai ébresztése)

You agree with cables, bridges and friends of old,
life is an anxious adventurer anywhere you go.
You had faith in the permanence of your faith.
Last week in Kassa* they repainted the rooms
of the house where you were born.

"Sir, what is your favorite color?"
 asked the painter, and you shrugged:
"Color it with life."
 Valér, the author—you recall the novel,
 the drawer ignored, the six-shooter,
 with one shell missing,
 the next one snuffed out your colleague's life—
 it was in the police report;
 the conscious half of reality got mixed up with a dream,
 the suspicion turned itself into fact,
 a magic potion that
 helps inspiration to add and subtract;
 but by the force of destiny
 can one subtract one's self from oneself?
 You maintained writing was magic,
 holy humility,
 the wild flood of unbridled rivers,
 in its stream the colorful bits and pieces of life,
 carrying with it the blinding glow of the universe,
 ignoring all ailments and plagues,
 time waves a hand from a smoldering train,
 if you keep your eyes on it,
 gives you a backward glance as an eddy;

if you forget to turn away,
an unknown body reaches out and snatches you
to its desert land, where there's no pain,
nobody hurts you;
under the ruffled arcades of the night
only the dream-hungry world is the watchman.

Don't rest in peace!
This world has become speedier and crazier
since your pains banished you far away.
Sharp blades light up every street corner,
and although peace
has been declared,
trees, too, sweat fear under the skin.
With teeth chattering
the future is shivering among mounds of snow,
from the elevated seat of skeptical view
the floundering of live reality seems theatrical.
Someone trying to break free of the net of reason
radiates mercy,
sketches a spotty map
on the hard-drive of consciousness.

The slither of shipwrecked sentiments
on the shores of hope is a new attraction
in the everyday life of the brewers of San Diego.
Those ready to sacrifice everything
for an hour of leisure
gather there
on the sand dunes of possibilities.
Despair draws

dark lights around them
at the bottom of a bloodshot sky,
and shadows scurry over their open arms
to taste the horizon.

Wake up! Create a sunrise!
Use words for armor;
writing is unbridled, watch for that wild river!
Be a traveler, the wanderer of oceans wide;
you can bring your life back to life with the help of life!

*Sándor Márai (1900–1989), one of the most important Hungarian novel-
ists, was born in 1900 in Kassa, Hungary, now Kosice (Slovakia). His novels
are bestsellers all over Europe. After the Hungarian Revolution in 1956,
he left his country to live successively in Naples, New York and San Diego,
where he ended his own life in 1989, just months before the collapse of
the Soviet Empire. Since then he has been widely published in Hungary,
as well as all over the world, starting in Germany, where the revival of
his works began. His influence has been well felt in the past thirty years
in Hungarian prose. He was the first writer to review the works of Franz
Kafka. Interestingly, like Hemingway, he chose to die by a bullet in the head.

HOLIDAY FEVER

(Ünnepi láz)

> *if the heart, if the heart,*
> *if only the heart stopped that rattle*
> —Domokos Szilágyi* *The Book of the Old*

the heart is rattling
celebration is no trivial matter
you need an occasion
    (an occasion that may or
    may not put you in the mood)
if something is about to commence or come to an end
it also holds in itself the holiday
in which doubt
and invention
the opportunity
to invite the gods
like in the Greek tragedies
let them glisten like gold nuggets like
salt rocks brought up from the mine
when they meet with sunshine
and playful time smiles at them

the body too adapts to the holiday
chests swell up
spines become ramrod straight
although clumsily nature too pitches in
even helps with the memorial service
it rolls out the fog curtains of alabaster dawns
in front of the occupants of the stage
on the blinking screen hung in space
it plays back the cavalcade of memory tatters
    (replaying what cannot be replayed)

we must let the tension dissipate

its good general well-being

the play-acting

mortals see a show like this only once in a lifetime

if they live to see that one

    (nobody forces them to

    take the bus to the bullfight in Acapulco

    at four in the afternoon in tired heat

    even one show is too many

    disgusting slaughterhouse

    bloodbath drowned in cruelty

    the joyless drops of fear lashing the windowpane

    on the other hand

    this too is a kind of holiday)

desire plays Judas

indecision in shards is a warm comforter

covers you with unlikely blue

the way the sky and sea used to wiggle

for eyes hungry for spectacle

reeling heights and depths on the retina of imagination

a holiday logo

coming from nothing to sing of its woe into nothingness

*Domokos Szilágyi (1938–1976), Hungarian poet of Cluj, Transylvania.

REMEMBERING KOLOZSVÁR
(Kolozsvári emlék)

Homage to Sándor Kányádi*

I hold out my arm,
a memory grabs my glance,
a checkered red-and-black
unselfconscious dance.
Fire-red solitude
drowning in my heart,
holds again inside me
black cares very hard.
Doubts remain around,
impossible to forget;
happiness, if any,
is always a poor bet.

> *Teams of lads and circles of girls,*
> *roses on fire, field-flower curls.*

Mutely, hand-in-hand, in dimming light,
their beaming looks embrace in stray delight,
their lips let the blood drops of the sunset seep;
the rising moon makes hale wind-horses leap.

> Teams of lads and circles of girls,
> the flame of life around them whirls.
> In pure black parades the lad,
> in red light is the girl's face clad.

The banks of Szamos** are mute and wan.
Above the ripples a memory hurries on.

Reflected in it sad stars melt
a bittersweet and moldy scent.

Without the one who never danced
life was not worth to be chanced,
teams of lads and circles of girls,
roses on fire, field-flower curls.

Fire-red solitude
drowning in my heart,
holds again inside me
black cares very hard,
a checkered red-and-black
unselfconscious dance.
I hold out my arm,
a memory grabs my glance.

*Sándor Kányádi (1929–), one of the most famous and beloved contemporary
Hungarian poets. He is a major contributor to Hungarian children's literature.
This poem follows the pattern and style of a Kányádi's verse "Fekete piros fekete"
("Black and Red and Black"), those being the dominant colors in the folk art of
Seklerland (Transylvania).
**Szamos, a river that runs through Kolozsvár, an old Hungarian city, now
in Romania.

THE MAGIC RECIPE
(Mágikus recept)

Homage to Béla Hamvas*

Monomaniacal, that's what I am, sir,
the representative member of an impossible generation
who's still on talking terms with Romanticism,
that artistic style. (There's no way I can get
away from it.) The search for the essence of going
bankrupt is an activity that defines my existence,
my natural state of being, the only way to my fulfillment.
But I'll continue to pay attention to you, sir,
I take your advice, I think about all that I've learned
from you, all that generations have copied
and quoted from you, shown off with before me
while stitching your victory on their triumphant
flag as their own.
The lack of spirit, too, requires a degree of intelligence,
the elegant gesture implied in the denial of everything is
not only a pose par excellence, but a way of life
in which the active half of imagination cuts itself off
from the indolent half and then passes
all of its functions to the latter.

You said it, sir, this will not make the world more athletic,
only sketchier, more fashionable and more rootless.
(Some call this state sacral madness.)

Directionless existence or vegetation in a rut,
call it what you will, is very chic nowadays.
It doesn't produce anything new, doesn't bother with it.

It simply vegetates—this is the new way to spirituality:
total immersion into nothingness for history-making energy.
(As we know, to splash trivial critical remarks into other people's
faces while one is vegetating is a pleasant way to pass the time.)

—As I mentioned to you earlier, sir,
I'm monomaniacal with a plaster cast on my brain,
a Calvinist—excuse me—a nihilist, the lurking
illusion of twisted forms and a displaced character
who believes the mood of the masses is easier to gauge
than its spiritual needs and disposition.

—Look, I've taken off the mask. My face is bare.
This the way I look. Have I earned your approval?
I'm far past the pivotal question of reality.
My power lies in the soul. (Laboring mounds of meat!)
My needs are modest, monomaniacal,
I cannot entertain you with trivia about myself.
Lacking in talent, on rare occasions I can create order
out of the jumble if I'm not too drunk,
but the thing is, I live in a world drunk on power (confusion),
and I'm facing an apocalyptic future (I already regret
having written all this, because the concept may tip over, and
some people may take offense); I breathlessly long for life,
I'm putting my private affairs in order, this is my craziness,
the great disorder I inherited; humor lives on a higher level
than tragedy, even though in front of the curtain or behind it
both genres represent the same force (if they behave themselves),
they both start by laughing at themselves.
I, too, laugh at myself, my dear sir, because I am laughable,
my life is a minor tragedy, and I am chronically fickle

(tyrannical), and I have been and will be, even if time (space-time)
kneels down with me, I monomaniacally keep licking reality
as if it was a popsicle.
How bitter!
Heaven has taken refuge behind imagination.
Maybe it knows something about which
I haven't got the faintest idea. For the time being. Tomorrow a
(Wall Street) shark will devour me for sure. I can hear the cries
of moralizers filtering in from the stream of auditory delusions;
from tatters of their words I conclude: people driven by hope
are a public menace (bandits?).
They want to fool this abnormal world.
They have the smarts to do it,
and the money, the time, the energy—and a keyhole.
What is that last thing for?
Through that they can spy on the fantasists,
the lawless elements,
the inquisitors and, of course, on me.
(I receive all this info with a leaden-gray face.)
"L'amor che move . . ." Let us love God! Love until we faint!
But what is God going to do with all that love?
Isn't it hard for him to stomach our hypocrisy?
Doesn't the overdone adoration disgust him?
Doesn't he suspect ulterior
motives behind pious words like requests,
personal interest instead of selfless, pure self-revelation?
Has faith turned into business?
It's for the desperate, the demented, the spiritually handicapped
to weave garlands for you from joy. (Love the sophists!)

I'll nurture in me the passion,

let my dear little saint grow big, that's my dream.

(Succubae, demons, phantasms in a single-person

mythology. None of what is happening to us is true.

Only the next generations will understand our dreams.

Actually, we dream our dreams for them.)

Life only requires more passion to be lived,

and then the magic recipe is ours. (The madman is only

a normal person who has seen a mentally healthy person

tell a lie. We don't have to change the world,

only deny it. You know that only too well!)

The impulse, the spastic clinging, serve the cohesion of

the universe, and so does monomania.

---

*Béla Hamvas (1897–1968) was a Hungarian writer, philosopher and social critic. He was the first thinker to introduce the Traditionalist School of René Guénon to Hungary. In addition, he was a great essayist who integrated Eastern and Western traditions, as well as posing many serious questions about the modern age, together with proposals for resolving them. One theory of his holds: *The present eon, since 600 B.C., stands in the sign of personal salvation. Only since this time has there been a notion of humanity, because there is only one single collective category of personality, and this is humanity.*

The author makes a strong allusion to the fact that privileged Hungarian writers during the Communist Era cited Hamvas's works and used excerpts from them as their own. Péter Esterházy was one of them.

IN THE CORRIDORS OF HISTORY

(A történelem folyosóin)

> *. . . Fine, may you be*
> *happy forever. Someday you'll*
> *regret having left me.*
> —Aladár Lászlóffy,* "Contemporary"

God uses the poet, too, to get his message out,
to get his wishes sensed throughout the ether,
to create the seasons of poetry
designed to redeem the words,

> what made some things magnificent
> was the ability to expect something
> from nothing,

the hand, the pencil, the shadow make me write these lines,
three of us are greeting you from the Longobard Era,
from the foothills of Umbria in fresh sunshine,
Deacon Paulus wipes the perspiration off his forehead,
and then he scans the faces around him in case he missed
something worth recording in his diary
that he may be queried about later

you
and
me

> in place of the sunken words now
> new words have come alive

and are already running through the corridors of history,
calling for a new parliament;

humanity must provide new proof

(if the proofs provided so far are insufficient)

they stop the unstoppable,

and in their impatient, pivotal effort

they again nail the Ten Commandments to the sky.

(Marry my dream so that I can sleep with you.

I promise to put aside indifference, irony and exuberance

and only focus on Botticelli and Galilei.)

The cyclist pedals unsuspecting,

like many other times,

sinking into hope up to the axle

(deep in thought: he'll reorganize the revolution

and everything else he constantly feels he must

reshape, reform, urge on

and publicize to the world)!

I am this cyclist,

merrily pedaling in summer

while daydreaming about you,

you with me

how nice it would be,

leaning into the wind,

two of us treading bicycle pedals

on our way, uphill,

facing outer space.

*Aladár Lászlóffy (1937–2009), one of the most important Hungarian poets.
 His legacy is everlasting.

UPDIKE

(Updike)

To John Updike, midnight, Wednesday, January 27, 2009, on the day of his passing.

Good heavens, what kind of mortality

does creation have for us?

For me, and you too, Updike,

whom I used to regard as a special envoy of immortality.

Your image lies before me on a fresh green lawn,

in the shade of sun-drenched mountains.

I reach out and feel your contours.

I lay my feverish hand on your chest, as if to ask,

Are you still alive?

Am I disappointed? Cheated out of something?

You vulture!

You're a statesman of estates,

a robber baron dressed in bright light.

And you'll never have a more devoted,

more faithful follower than I, my dear friend.

Now I must betray a secret to you:

Those who invested you with floodlight in your life

were the false agents of putrefying time.

Look at me!

I preach a different prophecy standing before

your spiritual body laid out here on the lawn.

Power, in the sense of possessing, is only a mirage.

(But what am I doing, explaining the force

of an aroused Viking warrior to you,

my dear friend, to you, your blood-splattering willpower?)

Snap me up in your jaws and run off with me

to join the shades of this world without souls.

But if you try to devour me or plant

a tree of fear inside me, I'll laugh at you.

Why me, of all people? Good heavens!

Instead, come with me to the airport

and let's greet there the grandchild arriving from Dallas.

There's a plane flitting across the delirious sky

and on the blue of your eye,

spreading fog as it flies on its belly.

What if it were to explode, scattering slivers of love?

My dear friend, you've deceived me!

You left me here in my Barbados solitude,

where even the Concorde no longer flies.

And yet I would so much like to take a ride

on the New York subway,

traveling with you

in the company of that wondrous creature,

that slender girl who almost invites a man

to reach under her dress,

slither a hand between her moist, warm thighs,

and extend a finger in her pants, shouting:

All's well with the world!*

You still sniff the scent of life,

don't you?

*Updike often made the New York subway the locale of his stories and never ran
away from sexual daydreams.

LOVE IN VENICE

(Szerelem Velencében)

In memory of Thomas Mann

I passed through Munich the other day,
strolled on Prinzregentenstrasse
holding my dear lady's hand
and wondering how Gustav von Aschenbach*
would feel looking up at the sky.
Would he see clouds in ruins
with blood seeping out?
Would he take refuge in another vision,
in the foliage of trees rooted in the flesh of the air?
Let memory do my work,
the favorites of the gods, the little phaias.**
Suffering, pleasure, sorrow, objectless longing.
His knees.
He rubs his legs; who wouldn't like to do the same?
But he's no Tadzio.*** A love of a later date.
The passionate revelation
of unfulfilled desire.

The soul is prone to witticism
when rummaging among painful things.
It enchants you, initiates you into
artistic illusions, testifies to belief
in words and spiritual journeys.
The man looking so handsome from a distance…
he was out there on the playing field this afternoon.
His strokes, the way he runs, walks and trips,
the spring in his step, his landing on his feet, are all gorgeous.

I couldn't have enough of watching him.
Dear youth, I must rest now. In truth
I wish for death, because I cannot bear
this longing
for the "divine child"...
This is how the essence perpetuates itself. It's propped up
by faith in beauty.
But, Master, if instinct and impulse,
the always and never,
build tunnels in the soul;
what is beauty?
Is there a resemblance between trees and stones?
Are two different things the same if they look the same?
Is it the same to see something and to make it seen?

Love is—science. Master, you put it just right.
You cannot work on immortality
if you tire easily. Love constructs
and devastates. Using both hands,
it destroys at night what it builds by day.

The wind from the sea is
blond mud; it plasters one grain of sand
to another.
Fancy and the universe go hand in hand.
Beauty labors tirelessly in the court of Eros.
Let your walk on the ocean beach be a happy one.
Take Tadzio with you, think about Phaidros,
a favorite of Socrates.
Writing too is delirium.
The flames of burning stakes.

One strains to catch it,

to hoard the enormous fire in his bowels.

Let us call this world-shaking,

self-generated and self-defined

eternal being

simply love.

* The main character in Thomas Mann's novella *Death in Venice.*
**"Theseus slew the sow at Krommyon called Phaia after the old woman who
kept it. Some say its parents were Ekhidna and Typhon."—
Pseudo-Apollodorus, *Bibliotheca* E1.1 (Greek mythographer C2nd A.D.)
***Tadzio, the boy Aschenbach falls in love with in the novella named above.
The lines in italics are from Thomas Mann's *Diaries,* except for the last two,
which come from Plato's *Symposium.*

FOR GÉZA SZŐCS'S SIXTIETH BIRTHDAY
(Szőcs Géza hatvanadik születésnapjára)

> *The poet likes to play a game,*
> *Harder and harder he plays*
> *Until he begins to feel the pain,*
> *Still much less than he betrays.*
> —Fernando Pessoa, "Autopsicografia"

who's that young man with a thick mane

waiting for someone on a mute street corner of Kolozsvár

he could be from the town of Vásárhely

that's how I know him

we met in Fellegvár

in the seventies (?)

around the diving tower we kicked the ball

(or each other's poetic feet)

and dreamed about the great Marinetti automobile

on the fresh green lawn

about Filippo Tommaso's *wild god of a steel people*

as he jubilates on the *whitening fingers of the big world*

like a *demented monster runs*

and flies over any everyday fantasy

the person standing on the street corner

in the cul-de-sac of inner endlessness

keeps an eye on the wind

around him a sliced world

retunes the present to the past

the rest is sunshine

glaze

it's too late when he makes a note of it

only the soul is snoozing

on the margins
of the paper
nothing-fort

life is a trousseau
keeps you on the go

and he was standing on a street corner of Kolozsvár
the young man with a thick mane
waiting for someone to return
with a hand held ready to caress
but it's all in vain
the Teddy Bear wracked by sobs
looking at Eva's grave

that's the life we face
Paris
a dying paraphrase

(a lyrical melody would fit here nicely)

to retune the present to the past
space-water floods the sidewalk fast
you can see that young man
who still uses ink to write
standing on the street corner in thought
writing the book of fate
having heaven wrought

(a moment of silence)

please forgive me for not recognizing you
in the Battle of Corinth

bitter joy radiated from your face
and in the heat of battle at one point you flashed a smile
but I didn't know what to do with it
one does what one can

> the wind is full of newsful news
> in my oven sings a goose
> I brought you a stone of ice
> and the light of heavenly device
> they pile up to my knee
> I can't leave as yet
> someone's looking for me

now it's me hanging out here on this street corner of Kolozsvár
waiting for you to appear on the cobblestoned sidewalk
conceding now it cannot be very easy for you
even if your dreams can fly in heaven and impromptu

(here I can hear Beethoven's string quartet in C Minor)

> to retune the present to the past
> space-water floods the highway fast

this was my wish for today

FIVE-STAR POEM DE LUXE

(Ötcsillagos luxusvers)

> Dedicated to Lawrence Ferlinghetti on the occasion of his
> acceptance and subsequent rejection of the 2012 Janus Pannonius
> Poetry Prize awarded by the Hungarian PEN Club

This is a five-star poem de luxe.
Smoking is not allowed anywhere inside.
They've given Bob Dylan and Ginsberg
the bum's rush through the back door.
Singing, though, is permitted:

Minnesota
we've lost it all
Saratoga
missed nature's call

Honey flows through the cavernous lobby.
Consciousness sits in club chairs.
Decided to stop
splitting.
Today.
They're marching Caucasian rams
(also permitted)
in the shade of solar flares.

Even Tandori* is getting bored
with the xylophone-phobic era,
yet he cheerfully keeps lecturing about existence
and the end thereof.
Why keep the universe on a leash,
let it be the other way around,
give me something sweet;
with that I'm never replete.

The sky of the eye can house
a tiny mouse.
Here only monomaniacal souls
are appreciated,
they get built into walls and battlefields,
fantasy can have a feast.
What about the specters? ask some in shock,
their genes need to be recoded,
no one wants this old malarkey,
peace is the key,
let it build a crest, dress up in high interest;
what kind of salt can call a halt?
(here it can make a cult!)
Go and keep fighting!

Uova strapazzate is the kitchen's hallmark.
The scent draws Manzonis and Flauberts
like flies.
But what about the specters? ask some in shock.
Mangia!

And what about the rest? What were they doing?
Resting their behinds in the library, reading Steinbeck:
"I can tell you folks are not from Oklahoma.
*I mean no offense, but you sound a little funny."***
Or perhaps Móricz:

> *"Those little rascals*
> *extended out a plank,*
> *and on its very edge*
> *they made him stand."*

. . . .

> *"No good, you crossed out another word.*

*You're writing a poem, aren't you?"***
and it amused him that smoking was banned in the smoking room
(and so was feeling cold in June).

Whoever tires of the peace below
can run upstairs and
watch a CNN show,
on the chairs coats hang,
a bottle of wine, 2010 vintage,
throw open the window, raindrops teem
in the room, they seem
to sound like Morse code on the floor,
with such force
that they awaken solitude
(if in the mood).

From this angle you can't see Dante's
house of birth,
pointless, ten years under renovation,
(a net around its girth)
chocolate-colored past.

Late memory. The breeze of evenings and air-conditioned trains
flit on fragile wings back into the past, lovely oblivion.
We owe you ideals and blood. The quiet misgivings of
our upturned faces, on their ruins snow-covered joy.
That's how we dream up morning, standing on its peak,
faint and scrawny ray, light stumbling on reason's lap.

The evening is memory, the air-conditioned train of clouds afloat.

Hotel Patagonia
greened by magnolia.

On the foothills of Torres del Paine you take a rest.
The constant silence will grow into momentum.
You document the excursion with photographs.
Dagger-thorns on the bushes of dreams.
(Smoking is not allowed there either.)

If one thing's not allowed,
nothing is allowed,
neither this nor another way
to create,
pointless to protest;
it'll be like that or not even that, no other way,
politics does not lord it over you,
the word falls under the barricades of the spirit,
János Csezmiczei was right when he sang:
"At a tender age I was sent by the land
of Pannonia where the Drava river cuts
across rich farm fields with slowing whirls
*to meld its waves and name into the Danube."****
The tree of humanism has grown tall
in the Hungarian land of Hunnia,
and so has Hungarian poetry;
sitting here we remain,
although badly beat up,
we have God light up our name.

*Dezső Tandori (1938–), Hungarian poet at the forefront of innovation.
**John Steinbeck (1902–1968), *Grapes of Wrath*
***Zsigmond, Móricz (1879–1942), Hungarian novelist, *Be Faithful Unto Death*
****Janus Pannonius (originally János Csezmiczei, Hungarian poet writing in Latin, 1434–1472), *Guarino-panegyricus*

DARK LIGHT

(Sötét fény)

Homage to Paul Celan

the glow of words is dark
the mind works in the dark
dark ice-flowers turn
to ashes brightly
the sun crosses the sky in the dark
the play of dark lightning
your confessions in a black box
in the dark bundles of time
misplaced mountains
shimmering on trees
dark leaves
road signs at intersections
black blank boards above
swinging over your head
in your dark room
black window frames
blind thoughts pace
up and down inside you
over your paper field
black lines
forming clouds of soot

ABOUT THE TRANSLATOR

Paul Sohar (1936–) drifted as a student refugee from Hungary to the U.S., where he got a BA degree in philosophy and a day job in chemistry while he continued writing and publishing in every genre, including seventeen volumes of translations, among the latest being *In Contemporary Tense*, Sándor Kányádi's poems (Iniquity Press, 2013) and *Silver Pirouettes*, György Faludy's poetry (Ragged Sky Press, Princeton, 2017). His own poetry: *Homing Poems* (Iniquity Press, 2006) and *The Wayward Orchard*, a Wordrunner Press Prize-winner (2011). Other awards: first prize in the 2012 Lincoln Poets Society contest and a second prize from Rhode Island Writers Circle prose contest (2014). Translation prizes: the Irodalmi Jelen Translation Prize (2014), Tóth Árpád Translation Prize and the Janus Pannonius Lifetime Achievement Award (both in 2016, Budapest, Hungary). Magazine credits include Agni, Gargoyle, Kenyon Review, Rattle, Poetry Salzburg Review, Seneca Review, and others.

ACKNOWLEDGMENTS

Grateful acknowledgment is expressed to the editors of the following publications where some of these translations first appeared:

Anomaly

Calque

Exit 13

First Literary Review-East

Loch Raven Review

Ragazine

Vox Populi

World Literature Today

CPSIA information can be obtained
at www.ICGtesting.com
Printed in the USA
FSHW02n0944030618
48783FS